What and Where

The Sound of WH

By Bob Noyed and Cynthia Amoroso

What? Where?
When? Why?
So many things
are in the sky.

Where does the sun go at night?

5

6

What makes the sky blue?

When does lightning flash in the sky?

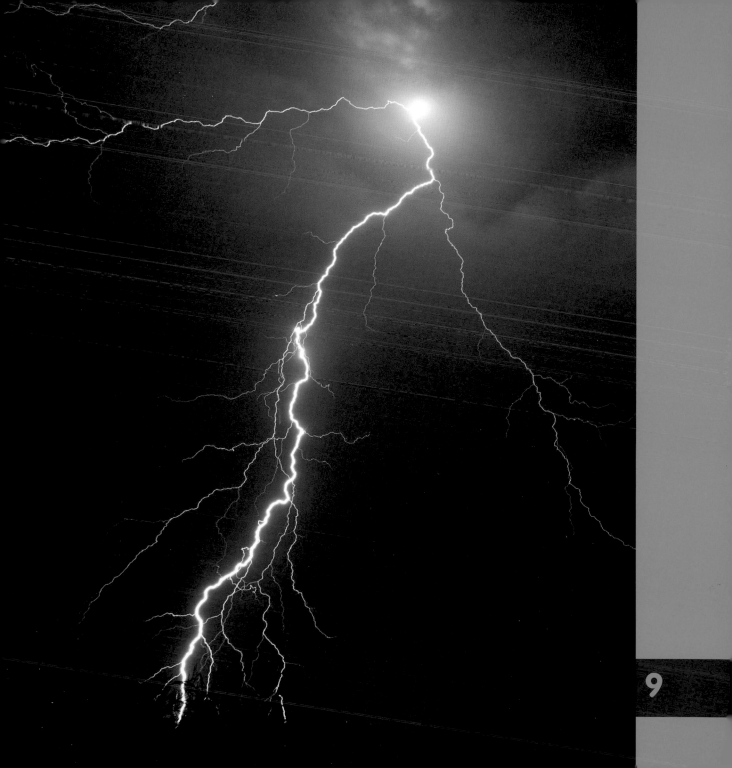

9

10

Why do the stars come out at night?

Where do rainbows end?

13

14

What makes the wind blow?

15

When is the moon round and full?

18

Why do clouds make rain and snow?

What? Where?
When? Why?
So many things
are in the sky.

21

Word List:

what

when

where

why

Note to Parents and Educators

The books in this series are based on current research, which supports the idea that our brains are pattern-detectors rather than rules-appliers. This means children learn to read easier when they are taught the familiar spelling patterns found in English. As children encounter more complex words, they have greater success in figuring out these words by using the spelling patterns.

Throughout the series, the texts allow the reader to practice and apply knowledge of the sounds in natural language. The books introduce sounds using familiar onsets and *rimes*, or spelling patterns, for reinforcement.

For example, the word *cat* might be used to present the short "a" sound, with the letter *c* being the onset and "_at" being the rime. This approach provides practice and reinforcement of the short "a" sound, as there are many familiar words made with the "_at" rime.

The stories and accompanying photographs in this series are based on time-honored concepts in children's literature: well-written, engaging texts and colorful, high-quality photographs combine to produce books that children want to read again and again.

Dr. Peg Ballard
Minnesota State University, Mankato

The Child's World®
childsworld.com

Published by The Child's World®
1980 Lookout Drive • Mankato, MN 56003-1705
800-599-READ • www.childsworld.com

PHOTO CREDITS
© Beth Swanson/Shutterstock.com: 21; Denis Rozhnovsky/
Shutterstock.com: 10; First Class Photos PTY LTD/
Shutterstock.com: cover, 2; irin-k/Shutterstock.com:
13; Jhaz Photography/Shutterstock.com: 9; jokerpro/
Shutterstock.com: 14; Liliya Linnik/Shutterstock.com: 6;
Mykola Mazuryk/Shutterstock.com: 5; NAAN/Shutterstock.
com: 18; Voraorn Ratanakorn/Shutterstock.com: 17

ISBN 9781503819313
LCCN 2016960524

Printed in the United States of America
PA02337

ABOUT THE AUTHORS

Bob Noyed started his career as a newspaper reporter and freelance writer. Since then, he has worked in school communications and public relations at the state and national levels. He continues to write for both children and adult audiences. Bob lives in Woodbury, Minnesota.

Cynthia Amoroso holds undergraduate degrees in English and elementary education, and graduate degrees in curriculum and instruction as well as educational administration. She is currently an assistant superintendent in a suburban metropolitan school district. Cynthia's past roles include teacher, assistant principal, district reading coordinator, director of curriculum and instruction, and curriculum consultant. She has extensive experience in reading, literacy, curriculum development, professional development, and continuous improvement processes.